T H E   P O C K E T   B O O K   O F

CARD GAMES

AN OUTLINE PRESS BOOK

Published by Chartwell Books
A Division of Book Sales, Inc.
114 Northfield Avenue
Edison, New Jersey 08837

This book was designed and produced by
OUTLINE PRESS

Design: Sally Stockwell
Illustrations: Peter Owen
Photography: Nigel Bradley

CONTENTS

INTRODUCTION

 Playing cards in one form or another are known in most parts of the world. They are used to play an enormous variety of games, from the simple and amusing to those that challenge the memory and agility of the mind.

Like dice, their eternal attraction is the chance element they introduce to a game. As with dice, it is the challenge of pitting one's skill, memory and intelligence not only against other players, but against chance. Chance introduces risk. To gain most one must often risk most. The successful weighing of odds and practice of judgement is both entertaining and satisfying. It is the basis of excitement in all good gambling games.

It is our aim, in this book, to provide the reader with a variety of games to suit most occasions – a patience game to pass the time if you are on your own, something to amuse the children or to entertain a group of adults. Many of these games have been played for hundreds of years. Over time and in different places, rules and terms are changed so that the same basic game may be played in several different ways. We have tried to relate the most popular version of each game included here, but we have not tried to cover all card games – Bridge, for instance, takes time to learn and there are many books written on that one game alone. The games in this collection are easy to learn and quick to entertain.

To begin with, play a dummy round or two of the game while reading the instructions and do not score or play to win. Once everyone understands how to play, begin in earnest. Where more than one pack is needed we will tell you. We also state where it is necessary to leave Jokers in play.

It will help you to know the following terms used in explaining the games:

Shuffle: To mix up the cards so they are completely at random and in no sequence or order whatsoever.

Trumps: A card or a suit that ranks above others for one game or as specified. The word derives from the old card game of "Triumph".

Tricks: The cards played in each round, one card from each player.

Wild Cards: Cards that can represent whichever other card a player wishes them to represent.

Stake: A bet or token.

Dealing: Distributing the required number of cards to each player. The easiest way to decide who is to deal is for each player to cut the pack. The person with the highest card wins the deal. Some games have definite rules of how to choose a dealer and where they do this is explained.

GAMBLING

 The dictionary defines gambling as the playing of games of chance for money. This may be so, but it does not mean that any of the following games have to be played for money. Indeed, it is in fact quite the opposite. All these games can be equally well enjoyed when they are played for points. Use matchsticks, paperclips, plastic chips or anything that can be used to score and which can change hands. You will have just as much fun and excitement trying to win, and great satisfaction if you do.

<hr>

THE ORIGIN OF PLAYING CARDS

 It has been suggested that European playing cards originated in China or India, but the most positive evidence shows them to have come into Europe through Italy from the Middle East. The Chinese and Indians have certainly known playing cards for at least as long as Europeans have, but theirs are quite different from ours. Whereas, cards of Islamic origin exactly like ours have been found from the thirteenth-century Mameluke world. Part of a twelfth-century pack of definite Islamic origin can be seen in the Topkapi Saraya Museum in Istanbul.

John of Rheinfelden, a Dominican friar writing in Switzerland in 1377, described the game of cards in detail and the pack as we know it now. An Italian called Giovanni de Covelluzzo, writing a hundred years later, says: "In the year 1379 was brought into Viterbo the game of cards, which comes from the land of the Saracens and is called by them Na'ib." Another Giovanni, but this time Giovanni Morelli, writing in 1393, mentions "Naibi" as a game. The Spanish, with their long Moorish history, still call playing cards "naipes".

So, it seems highly likely that cards came to Europe from Arab lands in about 1377. The irony is that Islam forbad the game because of its association with gambling, so cards used in the Middle East today tend to be European.

GAMES FOR ONE PLAYER

─────────────── *CATHERINE WHEEL* ───────────────

 For this game you need two packs shuffled together. The aim is to build sequences in a suit, descending from 5 to King and ascending from 6 to Queen, omitting the Jacks. Remove the 5s and 6s and lay them out as shown to form your foundations. Start with 5s and alternate the suits thus:

♦ ♥ ♦ ♥ ♣ ♠ ♣ ♠

Now deal the top four cards from the pack and lay them face up beneath the Catherine Wheel. Any card that can be added to the wheel goes straight into its place – Jacks are laid out following the 6 Spades, the Jack of Diamonds first, followed by the Jack of Hearts, etc., in the usual suit sequence. A 4 Hearts would go on a 5 Hearts followed by 3 Hearts, 2 Hearts, Ace of Hearts and King of Hearts. A 7 Diamonds would go on 6 Diamonds, followed by 8 Diamonds, 9 Diamonds, 10 Diamonds and Queen of Diamonds.

The minute you have an empty space in your row of four, fill it from the pack. If you can't play any of the four, start dealing face up from the pack into a discard heap. As a playable card or Jack comes up on the heap, put it in place. Constantly check the row of four to see when one of these can be played and fill the space at once.

You have to concentrate hard not to miss a playable card and not to start ascending on a pile that is descending. It is not easy, but it is great fun and very satisfying when you finish a Catherine Wheel with all the court cards on top.

ALL FOURS

Played with one pack, this patience game is ideal for children. It will show them the challenge and amusement that can be had from a pack of cards, even when there is no one to play with.

The aim is to get all the cards of the same value together in consecutive order. Shuffle the pack well and deal out thirteen piles with cards face down as shown – five to the top row, another row of five, and bottom row three.

The first pile represents Aces (1), the second 2s, etc., with the bottom row being Jacks, Queens, Kings.

Next, take the top card off the first pile. Look at it and place it face up below the pile with which it corresponds, i.e. 5 under the fifth pile from the left, 9 under the ninth (second from right on second row), King under the last, etc.

Now take the top card off the pile under which you have placed the first card and repeat the procedure. Go on like this until no more cards remain face down and you have all the Aces in the first heap and all the Kings in the last and the other numbers in their corresponding piles in consecutive order in between.

You would think that it's so simple you could get it out each time. Have a go! Sooner or later you will find there is no top card to pick up. You are then stuck, but you are allowed one chance. Carry on with the first face-down card from the left. If you get stuck again, that ends the game. Count all the cards that remain face down. This is your target to beat in the next hand.

THE LITTLE WINDMILL

 Take the four Aces from a pack and put them face up in a pile. Deal out the next eight cards to form a vertical and horizontal cross, as shown in the picture, with any 2s being placed diagonally between the arms and uprights of the cross.

The aim is to build four ascending sequences on top of these 2s. It does not matter what suit or colour, it is just the numbers in ascending order that count. Take from the cross and build up 2, 3, 4, 5, etc., on each 2. If you can't move, deal into a discard pile. Always fill the vacant spaces in the cross from the top of the discard pile, or if this is used up, then from the top of the pack.

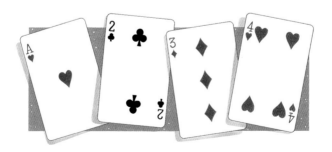

You should end up with the arms of the Windmill gone and the four piles set around the aces with a King on top of each. If it doesn't come out first time you may turn the discard pile once and play it through again. If you are concentrating properly, this is a very easy game.

--------------------- *ACE-TWO-THREE-FOUR* ---------------------

This is an excellent patience game, but it is not easy and requires concentration. To begin, put down any Ace, 2, 3 and 4 as shown:

The object is to build on each card, in the multiples of their value, so that each stack finishes with a king on top. We will call these the master stacks. Thus the sequence for each stack is as follows:

Ace (1)	2	3	4
2	4	6	8
3	6	9	Q
4	8	Q	3
5	10	2	7
6	Q	5	J
7	A	8	2
8	3	J	6
9	5	A	10
10	7	4	A
J	9	7	5
Q	J	10	9
K	K	K	K

Start the game by dealing four cards from the top of the pack face up underneath the Ace-2-3-4. If one of these cards can be used, in sequence, to start building a master stack, then do so. When no more cards can be used deal the next four from the top of the pack. Put them down on top of those previously played but leaving the tops showing of those that have gone before. This is important. Columns will build up under the Ace-2-3-4 like this:

If a column is emptied, then one of the bottom cards from the three remaining columns can be moved up to fill the space, thus revealing another possible card to carry on the sequence of building the master stacks.

Play continues until all the cards have been dealt out in groups of four. When you can play no further, count how many cards are not on the master stacks. This is your target to beat in the next hand. If you are lucky and clever, you will have the Kings showing on top of each master stack and none left on the table. It is possible!

Take a full pack of cards without jokers. Deal out four cards in a row face up from the top of the pack. Aces have the highest value, then Kings, then Queens, etc. The highest value card in each suit beats lower valued cards of the same suit, and these are removed from play. For example, if the first deal is:

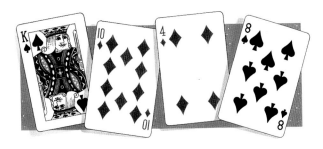

then the 4 Diamonds and 8 Spades are removed from play.

The next four cards are then laid down, in the same spaces as the first four, but leaving the tops showing of those cards still on the table.

The aim of the game is to deal out the whole pack four at a time, but at the end only have the four Aces left on the table and all other cards in the discard pile. When a space becomes available in the first (top) row, a card can be taken from the bottom of a row and moved up to fill the empty space.

Only the four cards with their full face showing have any killing power and a card can not kill a card it covers. So, in the example above, the Ace of Spades can not kill the King in its present position. However, the Queen of Hearts can remove the 2 Hearts and the Ace of Spades can move into the vacant position. The King of Spades can then be removed and the Queen of Hearts moved up into the vacant space.

Play in each turn comes to a standstill when you have one card of each suit showing. The next four cards are then dealt.

When all cards have been played, add up how many are left on the table once you are at the point when no more can be removed. In the next hand try to get lower than this number. This is the challenge – with skill and lots of luck you can get as low as only four cards, the four Aces!

GAMES FOR THE YOUNG

Most of the games described in this chapter are simple to learn and quick to play. Some of them are extremely noisy and all are great fun.

―――――――――――――――― *CHEAT* ――――――――――――――――

Two packs of cards are shuffled together and dealt out face down to the players. Any number can play.

The player on the dealer's left takes any one of his cards and puts it face down in front of him, announcing its value as he does. He can, in fact, say what he likes. If he calls 4, the person on his left must pick a 5 out of his hand and put it face down on the table. In turn, the player on his left must produce a 6, the next a 7, 8, etc., through to King, then beginning again with Ace, 2, 3 and so on.

Obviously there will be times when you can't produce the number you are supposed to because you haven't got it in your hand. In these instances you quite simply and innocently put down any card you like and lie about what it is.

If someone thinks you have cheated, he says "Cheat". If he is right, you have to pick up all the cards on the table. If he is wrong, he does so.

The first person to get rid of all their cards is the winner and the person left sitting with the pack comes last.

You will soon see that a cunning Cheat player can do all sorts of things to make sure his opponents end up with the cards. He can put more than one card down at a time if he can, or fumble around and look awkward before putting down the correct card, so that someone makes a false accusation of cheating, and has to collect the cards. It might not be a proper card game, but it is great fun at children's parties.

—————————— *WILLY WILLY MY BIRD SINGS* ——————————

 This is a ridiculous but noisy and very funny game to play with small children. If there are three players, use nine cards (eg. three Kings, three Queens, three Jacks). If there are four players, use four Kings, four Queens, four Jacks, four Aces. If there are three of you playing, the object is to collect three of a kind, and if you have four players, four of a kind.

Shuffle the cards well and deal them out to the players. Each player looks at their hand and selects a card they wish to discard. In unison, all the players take their card and place it face down in front of them on the table. They then slide the card to the player on their left. At the same instant, all players pick up the card they are being offered and add it to their hand. They repeat
this ritual as often as is necessary. If, on lifting a card from the table to your hand, you see that you have achieved a full set of

Kings, Queens, Jacks or Aces, you must shout out "Willy Willy My Bird Sings".

There is absolutely no point in making this ludicrous statement in a relaxed manner, as it is highly likely that if you have a complete set, one or even all of your fellow players may have one too. On the contrary, you must blurt it out as quickly as you can, and it must be correct. If two players shout at the same time and one becomes tongue-tied, the other is the winner.

PELMANISM

An ideal game for any number of young players, this is also a good memory test for adults. If you want to play as a large group and make it more complicated, try using two or even three packs of cards. Take a full pack of cards, including Jokers, well shuffled, and deal them out face down in six rows of nine.

Each player takes it in turn to turn over two cards so they are face up for all to see. If he turns over two cards of the same value, he takes them and turns over another two. He can go on as long as he keeps finding pairs. If his two cards do not match, he turns them face down again, and the next person takes a turn.

The player to have collected the most pairs once the entire pack has been picked up is the winner. The person with the best memory and longest attention span will win.

OLD MAID

 Take a Queen from a pack of cards and put it aside. Shuffle the rest of the pack well and deal it out to the players. It doesn't matter how many people play.

All players then look at their cards, sort any they can into pairs and discard them on to the table, eg. two Jacks, two 10s, etc. The remainder are fanned and held in the hand so that the other players can only see the backs of them. The person on the left of the dealer offers his hand to the person on his left, who selects any card. If it matches one in her hand and makes a pair, the pair is thrown on the table. If not, it is simply added to her hand which is then offered (with the backs of the cards only visible) to the person on her left. The procedure is repeated, going on round the table until all the cards are paired except one.

Someone will be left sitting with an unmatched Queen. Some say that this person is the winner, but most say that the winner is the one to be without cards first and the loser, the Old Maid, is the one who is left sitting with the Queen. As long as you decide first, it doesn't matter which rule you play.

This is a simple whist game for children, which two to seven people can play. Use a standard pack of cards and deal seven cards to each player. The remaining cards are placed face down in a pile in the centre. The top card in this pile is turned up, and this gives trump suit for the first hand.

Play now begins. The aim is to win all the tricks. The person on the left of the dealer leads with any card. The other players follow and must play the same suit if they can. The person playing the highest value card wins the trick. If a player cannot follow suit, they can win the trick by putting down a card from the trump suit. If they do not have trumps either, they should put down anything, but preferably something of low value as they are going to lose the trick anyway.

The winner of the trick starts the next trick and so on, until all seven cards have been played. Anyone who hasn't won a trick is eliminated from the game.

The cards are gathered up and shuffled, but in the second round the dealer only deals six to each player. In the next round five, then four, three, two and only one in the end, if the game goes that far.

Whoever wins the most tricks in a round chooses trumps for the next hand and leads off. Players who win no tricks drop out on the way and sooner or later one player will win all the tricks in a hand. This player is the overall winner.

───────────────── *SPADE THE GARDENER* ─────────────────

This game is best played with no more than five persons. It is just like the game of Happy Families and is in fact the forerunner of that game. The advantage is that you don't need a special pack. The Aces, Kings, Queens, Jacks and 10s of any normal pack will do.

These cards each have a special name and the suits mark the families to whom they belong.

The King of Spades is the Gardener

The King of Hearts is the Good Man

The King of Clubs is the Policeman

The King of Diamonds is called Vicar Denn

A Queen is a Wife

A Jack is a Son

An Ace is a Servant

A 10 is a Dog

So the 10 Diamonds is known as Vicar Denn's dog, while the Queen of Clubs is the policeman's wife. This is all very easy to

remember and now play can start. Shuffle and deal the pack face down to the players. Each player can then look at their hand and sort the cards into families.

The aim of the game is to collect all four members of a family and, if you can, all the families. As soon as you have a whole family, it is put aside out of play and you carry on. The person with the most families is the winner.

The person on the left of the dealer starts by asking any other player for a card she wants, for instance: "My dear Gertrude", you say (not that you are likely to have a friend called Gertrude!), "Have you got the Good Man's Wife?" If she has she must give it to you, and you can go on and ask her or anyone else for another card. If she hasn't got it, it becomes her turn to ask you or anyone else for a card she wants.

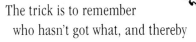

The trick is to remember who hasn't got what, and thereby deduce who must have what you want. There is also scope for a little play-acting – to make people ask you for something you haven't got, so that it becomes your turn. It can be a very funny game.

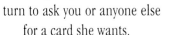

GAMES FOR TWO AND MORE PLAYERS

Cards can be fun in most games, but they are at their most satisfying when they allow the player to practise skill and where the outcome is not entirely dependent on chance. In this chapter we have chosen representative games from the world's most popular card game families, the reason for their popularity being the skill factor required to win. They provide a challenge and, once you get into them, they become most compelling. They are simple enough to teach to children, but have a content that makes them interesting and enjoyable to the most intelligent and ardent card players.

CRIBBAGE

Cribbage is a very old and excellent card game for two or three persons playing as individuals, or for four persons playing as partners. The pack of cards used is a standard pack of 52 cards, ranking from King high to Ace low.

The game commences with each player cutting a card from the pack to decide who shall deal first, the dealer being the person who draws the lowest card. The dealer shuffles the cards prior to each deal, the cards then being cut by the person to the dealer's right. With two persons, each player is dealt six cards, one at a time. The deal alternates between the two players after each hand. Each player looks at his six cards and lays away two of them to reduce his hand to four. The four cards laid away together constitute the Crib (or Box) which belongs to the dealer but is not exposed or used until after play. Next, the non-dealer cuts the remainder of the pack and the dealer turns up the top card thus exposed. This card, called the Starter, is placed face up on the pack. It is not used during the play, but if it is a Jack ("His Heels") the dealer pegs (scores) 2 points at once ("Two for doing it").

Play continues with the non-dealer laying one of his cards face up on the table in front of him. The dealer similarly places a card and play so continues alternately. As he plays, each announces the total of pips reached by the addition of his card to those previously played (eg. non-dealer begins with a 4, saying "four", dealer plays a 9, saying "thirteen"). The court cards count as 10 each. Every other card counts its pip value (Ace being 1).

During this play the running total of cards must not exceed 31. If a player is unable to add another card without exceeding 31, he says "Go" and play immediately passes to his opponent. His opponent may then continue to play from her own hand until she also is unable to play without exceeding the total of 31. The player of the last card pegs 1 point. Should the last card played bring the total score to exactly 31, the player pegs 2 points. When no further cards can be played without exceeding 31, the cards exposed on the table are turned face down and play is re-started by the player who did not lay the last card.

The object during this stage of the game is to score points by making the following combinations:

Fifteen: For adding a card that makes the total 15, peg 2.

Pair: For adding a card of the same rank as that played last previously, peg 2.

Three: For adding the third card of the same rank, peg 6.

Four: For adding the fourth card of the same rank, peg 12.

Run: For adding a card which, together with those played immediately before it forms a sequence of three or more, peg 1 for each card in the sequence. Runs are independent of suits but go strictly by rank eg. 9, 10, J is a run, but 9, 10, Q is not. A, 2, 3 is a run but Q, K, A is not. A run may be claimed whatever the sequence in which the cards were played, eg. in the course of playing 6, 7, 9, 8, the player of the 8 will score 4 points for completing the run, although not played in sequential order.

When all players have played all their cards in the above manner the cards are gathered up and scored in the following order: 1. Non-dealer; 2. Dealer; 3. Crib (Box). The scoring is calculated in the same way as during play with each player scoring combinations of Fifteens, Pairs, Threes, Fours and Runs. In addition, the following scoring combinations also apply:

- Each player counts as part of his hand, and also the Crib, the starter card which was originally turned up from the pack of unused cards. This inclusion gives each hand a total of four cards with which to achieve the various combinations.

- In addition to the scoring combinations described previously, points are also scored at this stage for achieving a Flush. This is achieved when all the cards in the player's hand are of the same suit (scoring 4 points), or when all cards in the player's hand plus the starter card are of the same suit (scoring 5 points). A Flush can only be scored by the Crib hand when it includes the Starter, and scores 5 points.

- A hand containing the Jack of the same suit as the starter card scores 1 point (for "His Nob").

Scoring with a Cribbage Board

A cribbage board is marked out with four rows of 30 holes, each divided into two pairs of rows by a central panel. The holes are grouped into sets of five for ease of visual reference. The normal length of the game is either 61 holes or 121 holes, being one or two complete circuits of each double row of peg holes and finishing with the game hole positioned centrally at each end of the board.

The winner is the first player to occupy the game hole, an exact score is not necessary. Scoring takes place by leap-frogging the cribbage pegs provided so that the leading peg always occupies that hole which represents the total number of points scored during the course of the game by the player concerned. It is customary to start scoring on the outer rows and to return towards the game hole on the inner row of holes.

Cribbage for Three Players

Each player plays for himself. The rules are precisely as for two-player Cribbage with the exception that each player is dealt five cards (not six) and one card is dealt to the Crib. Each player then lays away one card only to the Crib, so that the final composition of four cards for each player and for the Crib is maintained. Play always proceeds in a clockwise direction for the purposes of dealing, playing and counting.

Cribbage for Four Players

Here the four players play as partners, creating two teams. Five cards are dealt to each player, each player laying away one card to create the correct number of cards in players' hands and the Crib. Again all play proceeds in a clockwise direction. Each player plays and scores his hand on an individual basis but all scores count towards the team total, which allows considerable scope for cooperation at the playing stage and also at the stage of laying away one card for the Crib, where the choice will depend on whether the dealer is or is not a member of one's own team.

Playing for Stakes

It is customary to play this game for small stakes on the basis that the winner takes all. In these circumstances it is usual for a bonus payment to be made (by all players) to any player who scores 12 points (a Dozen) when the hands are counted. Such payment does not apply to a Dozen scored by the Crib hand. All stakes must naturally be agreed before the game commences.

─────────────────────── *EUCHRE* ───────────────────────

Euchre, or Euka, belongs to the Whist family of card games, as does Bridge. This has probably been the most played and most written about group of card games in the western world since the seventeenth century. In 1863, the editor of a revised edition of *Hoyle's Games* described Euchre as the most popular card game in the United States where, he said, it was considered to be the superior of Whist. It is still widely played in the USA and has a keen following in certain parts of Britain. Here we describe the Devonian game.

The game is played only with cards from the 8 to the Ace in each suit, plus the 2 Spades, which is known as the Benny. Only four people can play, in pairs, with partners sitting opposite each other.

The object of the game is to Euchre the opposition, which is to prevent them from getting the required number of tricks. The following are Trump cards and their order of importance:
1st: Benny (2 Spades), unbeatable whenever it is played
2nd: Jack of Trumps
3rd: Jack of same colour suit as the Jack of Trumps

4th: In descending order, Ace, King, Queen, 10, 9, 8 of Trumps.

Cut the pack to determine who is to deal. The dealer then deals two cards to each player, then a further three cards so they each have five (cards are not dealt one at a time, but in twos and threes only). The remaining cards are then placed in the centre of the table with the top card uppermost.

The player on the dealer's left may then say if he wants the suit of this top card as trumps. If he does, he tells the dealer to pick it up and discard another card from his hand. If this player doesn't want the exposed card as trumps the choice moves to the next player, which is the dealer's partner.

If the dealer's partner wants the card to represent trumps she merely turns it over. It is not picked up by the dealer. If she doesn't want it, the choice passes to the third player. If this player wants it the dealer must pick it up, but if he doesn't the choice becomes the dealer's. If he wants it he picks it up and discards, and the suit of that card becomes trumps for the game.

If the dealer doesn't want the suit to be trumps either, he turns the card over and, starting with the player on his left, players may call the trump suit of their choice. The first player to name a trump establishes that suit for the round.

No one may call the suit of the top card once it has been turned down. If no one calls trumps, then all hands are turned in and re-dealt.

If the top card is Benny, the dealer must call a suit "blind" – i.e. before he looks at his hand. This suit is then considered for trumps by each player instead of the top card.

If a player has a very strong hand or feels that he would do better playing without his partner, then he may tell his partner to turn in his or her hand. He gets extra points if he does this and succeeds in getting his required number of tricks.

Once the trump suit is decided, play begins with the player on the dealer's left leading. The object is to make at least three of the five tricks and all five if possible. If you don't make three tricks you have been Euchred by your opponents and they score.

Each player takes his turn to put down a card following the lead. You must follow suit if you can: eg. if a heart is led then all other players must play a heart if they can. If they don't have one they can play a trump to win, or if they don't have a trump they then just throw away their least valuable card. If Hearts are trumps and a player hasn't got any but has Benny or the Jack of Diamonds, they would have to play one of these as, you will recall, these are trump cards.

The highest card takes the trick and the winner leads to the next. Scoring is as follows:

If you make three tricks playing with a partner you get 1 point
If you make five tricks playing with a partner you get 2 points
If you make three tricks alone you get 2 points
If you make five tricks alone you get 4 points
If you Euchre the opposition and they are playing alone you get 2 points
If you Euchre the opposition and they are playing together you get 4 points

If you Euchre the opposition and you are playing alone you get 4 points

If you Euchre the opposition and you are playing alone and you get all five tricks, then you get 8 points.

The first couple to reach 31 points wins the game.

SEVEN CARD RUMMY

 This game uses two packs of cards including the Jokers. Any number of people up to seven can play. Shuffle both packs together and deal seven to each player. The remaining pack is put face down in the centre of the table and the top card is turned face up and placed beside it. The pack is known as the stock, the face-up card is the beginning of the discard pile.

The object of the game is to convert your hand into a sequence, a set, one of each or two of either.

A Sequence is three or more cards of the same suit with numbers in sequence. An Ace may be at the top or bottom of a sequence, as follows:

A Set is a collection of three or more cards of the same value regardless of suit, such as four Kings or three 9s.

All 2s and Jokers are wild and can represent any card the player wishes.

The person on the left of the dealer begins. He may pick up the exposed card on the top of the discard pile or may take the card off the top of the stock. His hand must remain at seven cards, so he must discard one card onto the discard pile. The next player then does the same.

As the game proceeds, players constantly change their hands and try to build them into sets and sequences. As soon as a player has all seven cards in sets or sequences they can be laid down on the table. This brings the round to an end and that player has no penalty points against him. All other players must now show their hands and total the value of their cards which are not in set or sequence. All court cards are valued at 10, aces as one.

A player can go down with only six cards in set or sequence as long as the seventh card is a 6 or lower, but in this case, that card will count against him.

A player cannot go down in the round in which he has picked up the card that completes his hand. He must discard as usual and wait a round.

The game is usually played with counters. At the beginning of each round the players each put a pre-determined number into a kitty. As each round is completed, points against are noted. When a player reaches 100 points he is out and no longer contributes to the kitty.

The remaining players play on until there are only two left. The kitty is then normally divided three to one, the three-quarters share going to the player with the fewest penalty points.

CANASTA

 Of all the games of the Rummy family this is probably the best and most exciting. It is an excellent game and can be played by two, three or four players in pairs.

As in Seven Card Rummy, players take from a pack or discard pile to change and build their hands, constantly picking up and discarding. Unlike Seven Card Rummy, you can build your hand openly on the table and secretly in the hand, and you may collect more cards than you started with if you can.

Again, two full packs of cards are used, with Jokers included. Jokers and 2s are wild and can be whatever you want them to be.

When playing two-handed each player has 15 cards.
When playing three-handed each player has 13 cards.
When playing four-handed each player has 11 cards.

The object of the game is to accumulate a hand with the highest points value possible. You usually play a series of games until one partnership or one player has reached 5000 points. Each card has a value and so do the different types of Canasta.

A Canasta is a collection of seven cards of the same value, eg. seven Queens or seven Fours. There are no sequences in Canasta. A Canasta with no wild cards is known as "pure" and one made up with wild cards as "impure". A Canasta built secretly and unseen in the hand is known as a concealed Canasta. Card and Canasta values are:

Joker	50 points each
Aces	20 points each
2s	20 points each
K, Q, J, 10, 9, 8	10 points each
7, 6, 5, 4	5 points each
Black 3s	5 points each
Red 3s	100 points each
All four red 3s in one hand	800 points
Impure Canasta	300 points
Pure Canasta	500 points
Concealed Canasta	600 points

Two- and Three-Handed Canasta

A dealer shuffles the packs, has them cut to him and deals the required number of cards to each player. The remaining pack is placed face down in the centre of the table, the top card is placed face up beside it to form the discard pack.

Players consider their hands and sort them into pairs of numbers (to start their collections of Canastas), into wild cards and into 3s.

Red 3s are immediately put face up on the table in front of the player and take no further part in the game except to affect the final score. They count as 100 points. The player then takes a replacement card from the top of the pack. This may happen at any point in the game when a player picks up a red 3.

Black 3s cannot be collected into Canastas. They are used solely for freezing the discard pack for a turn, in that they may not be picked up by another player when they are discarded. The only time they can be put down on the table otherwise is when a player is going out, in which case three or more can be put down.

The player on the dealer's left begins by taking a card from the top of the face-down pack and discarding any card face up on to the discard pile. Each player takes their turn to do the same.

In the first round, players may only take from the top of the pack. Thereafter they may take the discard pile – not just the top card, but the whole pile. They can do this only if they can meld, and go down on the table with part of their hand. A meld consists of at least three cards of a kind laid out on the table. A meld may have a wild card, but there must always be more natural cards:

two naturals, one wild

three naturals, two wild

four naturals, three wild = impure Canasta.

There can never be an equal number or more wild cards in a meld than there are naturals. Nor can there be a meld of wild cards only.

To go down on the table with the first meld in each game, a player must have a meld value above a certain threshold. In the first game this threshold is 50 points. In subsequent games it depends on the players' score. If they have accumulated 1500 points, the opening threshold is 90 points. If they have accumulated 3000 points, the threshold is 120 points.

This is a form of handicap and gives a distinct advantage to players starting with low scores from early games. It gives them a chance to catch up and adds to the excitement. An opening meld could look like this: The total value here is 60 points.

Once down, a player in their turn can add to the cards on the table or in their hand, constantly trying to build their score and make Canastas. They pick up from the top of the pack and place the card in their hand or add it to a Meld on the table. They finish their turn by discarding one card.

If the previous player has discarded a card you want, or there is something in the discard pack underneath that you want, you may take the whole pack on the following conditions:

- You have a meld of the last card discarded, eg. you have gone down with the above opener and the person on your right discards a King. You may simply pick the discard pack up, if it is your turn, place the King on the table (the top card must always go down) and put the rest in your hand, or add them to runs on the table, or make new ones if you want to.

- You have not melded and gone down yet but have two natural cards in your hand the same as the one discarded, eg. you have two Kings. You may then put them on the table, show that you can make the required 50 by putting down a meld such as the two 4s and the 2 and then pick up the discard pack, add the King to the 2 on the table and do what you will with the others. At the end of your turn you must always discard.

Capturing the pack is very important in the early stages of the game. It enables you to build up your hand quickly, the alternative being one new card in each turn. Because it is so important, a tremendous tension is introduced to the game, especially if you have seen people throwing things away that you really want.

To stop people capturing the pack, you have two options:

- The black 3, as described, cannot be picked up by the player to whom it is discarded. It therefore blocks the pack for one turn.
- A wild card, Joker or 2, when discarded does the same. It is placed sideways on to the rest of the pile, so as to stick out and be seen. But, a wild card freezes the pack so that no player can pick it up even if they have got a run of the subsequent top cards on the table. They can only pick it up if they have two naturals in their hand. These are put down on the table, the top discard is added to them and the rest of the discard pile is taken.

As Canastas are formed, the seven cards are closed up to form a small pile with a red card on top to signify a pure Canasta, a black card signifying an impure. A pure Canasta collected in the hand is put face down so that other players can only guess at its contents. An eighth card can be added to a Canasta.

Be sure never to leave yourself too short of cards in the hand. This will lessen your chances of being able to pick up the pack.

A player can go out and end the game when he has a pure Canasta plus one other, and all his cards meld. The player must pick up in his last turn, but does not have to discard. Wild cards can be added to runs and pure Canastas (but it makes them impure) and three or more black 3s can be put down on going out. The player going out gets 100 points.

Now, each person's score is added up as follows:

For going out: 100 points

For each Canasta: [300-800] points

For each red 3: 100 points

Then add the total value of melded cards on the table.

If you were not the player to go out, the total value of the cards in your hand is subtracted from the value of the cards on the table to find your score.

If you did not manage to meld and go down at all, any red 3s are counted against you with the cards in your hand. If someone goes out very quickly in a game, it is possible for players to be left starting the next game with a negative score. In this case they have no threshold to reach for a meld and may pick up the pack and go down with two naturals, even if they are two 7s and only worth 5 each.

Scores are noted and the next game commences. Play continues until one player or a partnership reaches 5000.

The Peculiarities of Four-Handed Canasta

When four people are playing they act as two partnerships and each partnership scores as one. Each person is dealt eleven cards and plays his or her own hand. Partners may not show each other their hands nor may they communicate save one question at the end.

Partners may build on each other's hands on the table. They may only do this when both have melded and gone down. So, if you have three 4s on the table and five Kings and you can see your partner also has three 4s on the table, you may take yours and add them to hers to make six. In her turn, if she has Kings in her hand, she may add them to yours. So, you work together to build up your score. You must try to show your partner what you need and try not to discard what she needs. A partnership may go out with only one pure Canasta, but it must be in the hand of the player going out.

If you want to go out and you can see that your partner is carrying a fistful of cards which will add to a huge negative, you may ask "Can I go out next turn please?" Whether the answer is Yes or No, you must abide by it. You must not begin a great discussion. If the answer is Yes, it gives the partner and the opposition a chance to off-load everything they can. You can then go out in your next turn. But, you don't have to ask. You can just go out and catch everybody.

Canasta is probably best played with four. It is a very different game tactically with two and three players. But, however you play it, it is exciting and thought-provoking.

♥ ♥ ♥ ♥

BRAG

 This is a very old gambling game which is probably the ancestor of Poker. It doesn't have to be played with money because it's a gambling game, but it is essential to have counters or matchsticks with which to bet. As ever, there are several variations of the game, but the most common is three-card Brag.

Decide at the start who is to deal and what the maximum stake is to be. Use a full pack of cards. Three cards are known as Braggers: Ace of Diamonds, Jack of Clubs, 9 of Diamonds. These cards are wild and can be whatever you wish.

A hand is valued in the following hierarchy:

1. Three of a kind: natural, Ace high, down to 2.
2. Three of a kind, including one or more Braggers.
3. Two of a kind: natural, Ace high, down to 2.
4. Two of a kind, including one or more Braggers.

If two players have similar pairs, the player with the highest third card wins. If no player has a three or a pair, the best single card wins.

Play begins with the dealer putting down a stake. He then deals three cards to each player. Once they have looked at their hands they must bet on the outcome. They must put out a stake at least as high as the dealer's to stay in the game. If they have nothing in their hand to give them confidence they may retire.

Play goes round the table and back to the dealer. If everyone has retired there is no game. If some players have matched or raised the dealer's stake it is now up to him. If he is confident he has a winning hand he puts down another stake at least as large as the stakes on the table.

Again, players around the table consider their position and confidence. They must retire and forfeit their stake, or put down a matching stake. If the dealer has a bad hand, he too may retire, leaving his stake in the pool.

When a player has bet an amount that no one else is prepared to match, the others retire and he takes the pool of tokens. He does not have to reveal his cards, so he could be bluffing and have nothing of any value at all, but still win.

If any or all players want to see a high-bidder's hand, they must first bet a higher amount and then call to see his hand. At this point all hands are revealed and the best hand takes the kitty.

You need nerves of steel and acting ability for this game.

BLACK MARIA

 Although it can be played with more, this game is best played with three players and is considered by many to be one of the very best of card games. Its appeal lies in the fact that players can practise their skill more in this game than in many others.

Remove the 2 Clubs from a normal pack and play with 51 cards. The aim of the game is to avoid taking tricks which contain any penalty cards. These cards and their penalty points are:

Queen of Spades – Black Maria	**13 points**
King of Spades	**10 points**
Ace of Spades	**7 points**
All Hearts, each of which carries 1 penalty point	

Shuffle and cut the pack for deal, the lowest cut becoming the dealer. The dealer then deals out the whole pack face down equally to the three players.

Players sort their hands into suits and sequence – Aces high. They then select the three cards they want least in their hands and pass them face down to the player on their right. They may not look at the cards they are receiving until they have chosen and passed the three they are discarding.

Play begins with the person on the dealer's left putting a card face up on the table. The next on the left must play a card of the same suit if she has one, and the third player must then do the same to complete the trick. If a player has no cards of the right suit he may discard any card of any other suit.

The trick is won by the highest card of the suit of the first card played (the suit of the leading card). The winner of a trick leads with a card to start the next trick.

Play continues until all 17 tricks are completed. Each player can then total the penalty points of the cards in the tricks they have won. The player with the least penalties wins the round.

Skill can be applied throughout this game in the passing of cards at the beginning and obviously in the play itself. Once you have played it a few times you will begin to appreciate all the options for cunning play.

CARD GAMES FOR FUN

These next few games can be enjoyed by any number of players and by any age group. They are ideal for parties. Although challenging and fun, they don't make you think too hard.

CHASE THE ACE

 Each player starts with three counters which represent his three lives. The object of the game is to make sure you are not the one holding the lowest value card in each round. If you are, you surrender a counter and lose a life. When you have lost all three lives you are out. The winner is obviously the person who remains holding one or more counters when all other players have lost all their lives.

The ranking of cards is as follows:
Ace is the lowest value and King the highest.
Clubs rank lowest in suit, followed by Diamonds, then Hearts, and Spades have the highest value.
So, the Ace of Clubs is the lowest possible ranking card and the King of Spades is the highest.

The dealer deals one card face down to each player, who may look at their card. Any player who has a King turns it face up on the table.

Now, beginning with the player on the dealer's left, each player who hasn't got a King may change his card with the player on his left, if he so wishes (unless that player has a King). This option is also available to the person on the dealer's right.

Once every player has decided to keep their card or has exercised their option to exchange it with the player on their left, then the dealer may decide upon his card and consider his move. He may keep his card, or cut one from the pack. Whichever he does, all cards are now revealed and the person with the lowest loses a life.

Each round continues in the same way. The cards are shuffled after each hand and the deal moves to the next player on the left.

PONTOON

Also called 21 or Vingt-et-Un, this is probably the most popular and simple of card games for a group of players. First, choose the banker by making each player take a card from the pack. The person with the highest gets the bank, which is not always an advantage. It should be, but if there is an experienced player present who bets high, he can cripple the bank quickly if he is lucky. For this reason it is a good idea to decide on a maximum stake at the outset of the game.

The banker starts by dealing one card to each player including herself. The players look at their cards and place a bet on the table before them. The bank then deals each a second card.

The aim is to have a hand with a total value as close to 21 as possible, or a hand of five cards with a value of 21 or less. Court cards are all valued as 10. Aces can count 1 or 11, as the player wishes. All other cards are according to their value.

A pair consisting of an Ace and a 10 or Court card is an instant winner; the cards add to 21 exactly and are shown face up on the table at once. This is known as a pontoon.

The other players keep their cards a secret to themselves. Starting with the person on his left the banker asks each person what they wish to do. Their options are as follows:

- A player can buy a card by putting out more counters. He may not buy for more than his original stake. A card that is bought is delivered face down by the banker.

- The player may decide to "twist" – ask the banker to turn over a new card – in which case there is no charge and the card is delivered face up for all to see.
- A player can buy or twist as he or she wishes once, twice or three times.

If a card brings the player's hand to a total value above 21 he is "bust", and this must be announced. The banker takes the stake.

When a player is satisfied with his hand he "sticks" and the banker moves to the next player. Once everyone has bust, stuck or got a pontoon, the banker plays her own hand.

The banker turns up both cards and can twist to add more cards if he or she wishes. Once the bank has decided to "stick", it pays out to anyone who has beaten it but takes the stake of those it has equalled or beaten.

For instance, the bank starts with a King and a 2. It turns another card, a 7, bringing its total to 19. It would be prudent to stop at this point, as it would be extremely lucky to get another 2 or an Ace and anything else would bust the hand. So, the Banker announces that she will pay 20 and up, and must pay accordingly:

Three times the stake for a pontoon.

Twice the stake for five cards of 21 or under in value.

Twice the stake for any cards adding to 21.

Once for any cards adding to 20.

All winning players obviously keep their original stake. If the bank busts itself, it pays out to everyone who is still left in the game. If the bank gets a pontoon it beats everyone outright.

If a player gets a pontoon, he takes the bank in the next round. If two players have pontoons, the bank goes to the first player on the banker's left.

<hr>
NEWMARKET
<hr>

 This is a wonderful game for families with younger children. You will need tokens or matchsticks, one full pack of cards plus the Ace of Spades, King of Diamonds, Queen of Hearts and Jack of Clubs from another pack.

The latter four cards are laid out face up. They are used as the base for the stakes. Each player must put down a stake on one or more of these cards before the deal.

The dealer then deals out all the cards, always dealing an extra, dummy hand, i.e. if there are four players he deals out five hands.

The aim is to use up all the cards in your hand and also, if you can, to play one of the four "luxury" cards – those equivalent to the ones with the stakes on them on the table.

The player on the left of the dealer starts. He looks at his hand and throws out face up the lowest card he has in any particular suit, and calls it as he does so. If it is 3 Clubs, whoever holds the 4 Clubs must follow. If you are in the ideal position of holding a sequence yourself (3 Clubs, 4 Clubs, 5 Clubs etc.), then you can play them yourself one after the other.

Play moves around, one player following another, until a card needed to follow is not in anyone's hand but is in the dummy. With this interruption, the same player continues, but she can start again with another card or another suit.

As soon as a player is out, the others have to pay him or her a token for each card in their hand.

During play, any player putting down a luxury card takes the stake on that card. Those stakes on the luxury cards that are not collected before the first person goes out remain to be added to for the next hand.

If everyone starts with the same number of tokens, the winner is the one with the most after a set time or a predetermined number of turns.

There is so much entertainment to be had from a simple pack of playing cards. Apart from these games, you can use them to fascinate your friends with card tricks or frustrate yourself by building card houses.

Whatever you do with them – have fun.

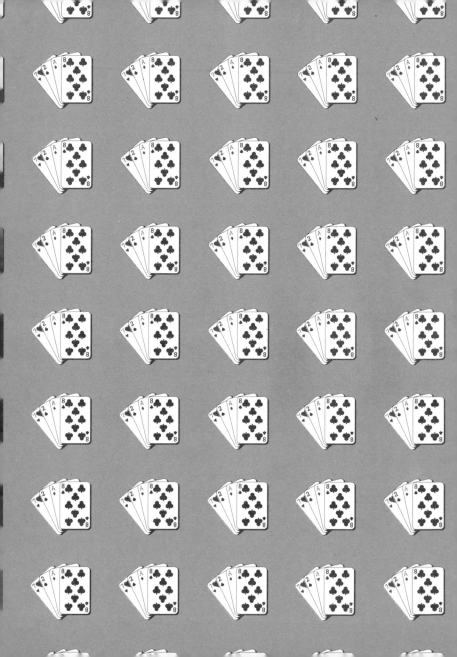